(place a photograph of your cat here)

Name _____

Address _____

Tel no. of veterinary clinic _____

Tel no. of local cat hotel _____

David & Charles

A DAVID & CHARLES BOOK

First published in the UK in 2003 by David & Charles

First published 2002 by David Bateman Ltd,
30 Tarndale Grove, Albany, Auckland, New Zealand

Copyright © Mary Trewby and David Bateman Ltd, 2003
Copyright photographs © Graham Meadows, 2003

Distributed in North America
by F&W Publications, Inc.
4700 E. Galbraith Rd.
Cincinnati, OH 45236
1-800-289-0963

ISBN 0 7153 1609 5

A catalogue record for this book is available from the British Library.

Printed by Everbest Printing Company
for David & Charles
Brunel House   Newton Abbot   Devon

David & Charles books are available from all good bookshops. In case of difficulty, write to us
at David & Charles *Direct*, PO Box 6, Newton Abbott, TQ12 2DW quoting reference M001,
or call our credit card hotline on 01626 334555.

Visit our website at www.davidandcharles.co.uk

Contents

MY name is

The name of my human companion is

We live at

I am a male/female cat

The type of cat I am is called a

My fur is short/long. The colour of my fur is

The colour of my eyes is

I was born on the _____ day of _____ [month]

in 20 _____ [year] at _____ am/pm

The name of the place I was born is _____

MY mother is _____

MY father is _____

I have some brothers and sisters who were born at the same time.

They are _____

If you know your cat's pedigree/parentage, fill in the spaces above and place a photograph of your cat below. If you don't know about your cat's parents, fill in the spaces below and put the photo over the unused space above.

I don't know exactly when or where I was born.

I met my human companion at _____

We were introduced by _____

Cat ID

Your cat has a unique set of paw prints — unlike those of any other cat in the world. Take prints off the paws using a stamp pad of cotton wool and food colouring. Make sure that you clean the cat's feet as soon as you've made the paw prints in the spaces below.

Photographing cats

Not the easiest of subjects, except when asleep, cats are fast movers and require quick reactions on the part of the photographer. Photographing cats also requires patience. The reward — getting wonderful portraits and action shots of your cat — is well worth a little trouble, though.

For the best photos, spend some time watching your cat and learning its habits. Do it quietly so that the cat is unaware of your presence. After a while, you will know it so well that you may learn to anticipate its movements. When the time is right, be ready with the camera and have lens settings adjusted and focused so that you make the most of your chances. It is important to correctly expose for the cat rather than the surroundings.

Use fast film. If you have a long-focus lens, from 200 mm up, use it to get close, in-focus photographs. A motor drive means you don't have to rewind manually, but is noisy and could be disturbing.

You don't need to try for unusual effects. The best photographs are those that show your cat in a characteristic pose or movement.

Left front paw   Right front paw

(place a photograph of your cat here)

Left back paw

Right back paw

First impressions

Whether a kitten or older, your new cat will take a little time to get to know its new human companion. It will have to learn all about you — your looks, smell, voice, habits, family, regular visitors — explore its new home, and fit in to your schedule. It may have to make friends with family cats and other animals. For you, too, there's a lot of learning to do: you need to adjust to your cat's own particular personality and rhythms. Make a start by recording your first impressions of your new companion.

Description (colouring, size, hair type, etc)

Eating habits (what it loves, time between feeds, how much it eats, etc)

Play (favourite games, toys)

Other habits (climbing, rolling, etc)

Sleep patterns

First-night nerves

Expect your new cat to be a little nervous on the first night it spends with you. Make it comfortable by placing its bed in a warm spot and give it something soft and cuddly, like an old sweater or a soft toy, to curl up against. Some kittens like to hear the tick-tock of a distant clock, to remind them of their mother's heart beat.

Cats and dogs

A dog will accept a kitten more easily than an older cat. Introduce them gradually. Keep them apart on the first day, then let them get to know each other while you watch. It's best to have the dog on a leash at first so that it doesn't bark or become excited and scare the cat. Expect a few hisses and the occasional swipes with a paw — be ready to pull the dog away if necessary. Wait until they are used to each other before allowing the dog to lick the cat or get too close. It may take several weeks before the cat and dog have accepted each other's presence.

Cats and children

A small child finds a kitten very hard to resist. It has a tail that can be grabbed, ears to pull and fistfuls of fur. Always supervise small children around the cat. A young kitten may react to rough treatment with its claws. Teach children that the cat must be treated gently and with respect. And make sure they know the correct way to hold and lift the cat, and how to know when the cat wants to be left alone.

Introducing one cat to another

If you already have a cat, it is usually easier to bring a young kitten into the house than another adult cat. Allow the cat to sniff the kitten — there may be some hissing and growling at first. Then leave them to it. Only interfere if the cat attacks the kitten. Be sensitive to the older cat's feelings and make as much of a fuss of it as you do of the newcomer.

My new best friends are:

Your new cat

You can live with a cat for about as long as you live with a child — into the late teens or longer. So, whether your new cat is a kitten or older, you need to make sure that it is healthy and happy. And be clear you know exactly what your responsibilities are as a cat-owner.

The healthy cat-a-log

- A healthy cat has a firm, muscular body and feels heavier than it looks.
- It is lively, active and well nourished.
- Eyes are bright and clear with no discharge. The third eyelid isn't visible.
- Ears are clean, with no discharge.
- Its nose looks velvety and is cool and slightly damp.
- Mouth and gums are pale pink, and its breath odour-free.
- Its fur is soft and glossy, and smooth to touch.
- Limbs are straight, not bowed.
- Its abdomen is slightly rounded, but not pot-bellied.
- Its ribs do not protrude.
- Rear is clean, with no signs of diarrhoea or discharge from the genitals.
- Its tail has no kinks.

First vet visit

It's essential to take your new cat to the veterinarian for a check up, especially if you have other cats in the house. As well as giving your cat a full examination, the vet will schedule a series of vaccinations and, if necessary, administer a de-wormer. This is an opportunity to ask advice on cat care and training. Make sure you discuss reproductive issues, including neutering to prevent unwanted kittens.

Vital statistics

Date	Weight	Height	Body length

Deworming

Date	Type

Vaccinations

Find out what vaccinations (if any) the cat has had already. A vaccination certificate should be available.

Date given	Vaccine type	Batch no.	Veterinarian signature

Health notes

The cat corner and other essentials

Every cat needs a space of its own — a snug corner with a comfortable bed, where it can enjoy a little peace and quiet. Because a small cat tends to catch chills and respiratory infections easily, choose somewhere that is draught-free and keep the temperature at around 75-80°F (24-27°C).

Essentials checklist

- Separate food and water bowls.
- A cat basket or bed that is comfortable, warm and easy to clean.
- A litter box, which is kept clean.
- A carrier.
- Combs — fine-toothed to search for fleas, wide-toothed for grooming.
- A soft-bristle brush.

Your responsibilities as a cat-owner

Bringing a cat into your home will change your life. Although a cat is not demanding, you must be prepared to give it the care and attention it needs: a healthy diet, regular grooming, and proper health care. And, like all creatures, it thrives best when it has sympathetic companions who give it love, attention and join in with its games.

How a kitten develops

One of the joys of owning a kitten is watching it change and grow. As it learns to control and coordinate its limbs, it will begin to explore its immediate environment, learn patterns of behaviour, and stumble and pounce, run, play and jump. Once you understand what is going on, you can respond to these changes, helping the kitten grow into a happy, healthy cat.

From four to 12 weeks

The kitten will be able to handle solid food and should have been house-trained by its mother. You should start training the young kitten at this stage, and getting it used to its name and to the litter box. By around four or five weeks, it should have all temporary milk teeth (which begin emerging by the second or third week), and will be moving quite well. The average kitten of this age will weight about 1 lb (450 g), will be learning to groom itself, and playing with its siblings. The kitten should be fully weaned by about six weeks, although it will probably still try to suckle if it gets the chance. At nine to 12 weeks, it is appropriate for a kitten to move to a new home.

Dangers

- Be gentle when playing with the kitten — at 12 weeks it is still very fragile with soft bones and motor skills not fully developed.
- Do not leave small objects around — they can be swallowed.
- Keep your fireplace covered — the kitten may use the ashes as a toilet area, or disappear up the chimney.
- Always put down the lid on the toilet — an adventurous kitten could fall in and drown.
- Keep kittens away from electric cords — they are inviting to bite, and can cause shock, burns or even death.

Progress notes

From three to seven months

At this age, the kitten's motor coordination has improved, and it will be energetic, mischievous, and enjoying play and games.

It may find teething uncomfortable, even painful — signs are crying, low energy, loss of appetite and diarrhoea. The permanent incisors begin appearing at about three or four months, the canines at five months and the premolars at six to seven months. It is normal for the kitten's gums to be sore and perhaps bloody. The kitten may gnaw at objects to relieve teething pain — provide a tough piece of leather that cannot be shredded and swallowed.

Dangers

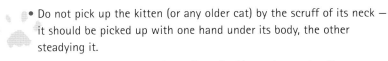

- Do not pick up the kitten (or any older cat) by the scruff of its neck — it should be picked up with one hand under its body, the other steadying it.
- Do not handle it too much — allow the kitten time to itself.

Progress notes

All kittens have blue eyes when they are born; if the eye colour is going to change, this will begin at about 12 weeks old.

Training

Hopefully, by the time the kitten becomes part of your household it will have learnt a great deal from its mother. Successfully training your cat to live happily as part of your family depends on balancing your own expectations with the cat's needs and nature. You have to learn how a cat communicates and understand the difference between normal cat behaviour and misbehaviour. Spend some time observing your cat. Find out what it likes and dislikes (for example, whether it likes being picked up and stroked or prefers to approach you in its own time), and tailor your training programme accordingly. The key to winning your cat's cooperation is gentleness and patience. Keep notes on your cat's progress.

Training methods

Consistency is important — reinforce good behaviour and express disapproval of unacceptable behaviour systematically until the cat learns to do what you want it to.

Rewards not punishment

The best way of teaching the cat to do what you want it to and discouraging misbehaviour is to reinforce good behaviour. Reward the cat with praise and affection, and perhaps with a food treat (never feed a cat immediately after it has misbehaved). Social reinforcement — stroking, tickling under the chin, games and praise — is also an excellent way of rewarding good behaviour.

Discourage unsuitable behaviour

Discourage the unwanted behaviour at the time it occurs — the cat will only associate a reproof with its current activity.

A firm but gentle 'No' command may be all that is required to discourage bad behaviour. A cat is highly skilled at interpreting differences in sounds, and will quickly learn the mood and tone of displeasure in your voice.

Use indirect means as discouragement, for example, water sprayed from a pistol (don't let the cat see you operate the spray) or a rolled newspaper tapped on the floor near the cat while saying 'No' firmly. In this way, the cat does not associate you with the reproofs and its good behaviour may not be dependent upon you always being present to enforce it.

Never strike a cat or display anger towards it. Pain and aggression have no part in any training programme.

Commands

A firm but gentle tone is essential for effective commands. Use one-syllable, single-word commands. Always use the same command for a particular activity.

Notes

Calling Your Cat

Choose a name for your kitten as early as possible — one that is easy for the cat to recognise. Repeat it whenever you are stroking the cat, when it is walking towards you and when you are putting out its food. The cat will soon make the connection.

Notes

Handling a Cat

Avoid picking up kittens too much — they are small and fragile. Do not pick up a kitten — or a grown cat — by the scruff of its neck; it is precarious and may cause pain.

Always support the cat's full body. Put one hand under its chest, the other under its hindquarters, and lift. Let it sit in the crook of your arm with its forepaws on your shoulders and supported by your other hand.

Toilet training

If it is not already trained, place the kitten in the litter box immediately after feeding and waking. Make scratching actions in the litter with your finger to show it how to dig. The kitten will generally catch on quickly — don't force it to stay in the box. If it makes a mess on the floor, never rub its nose in it. Instead, deposit the waste in the litter box — the smell should direct the kitten there next time. Praise and stroke the cat to reward it for correct toilet habits.

Do not place the litter box near the cat's food and water. Instead, find a location that provides a sense of privacy and safety, possibly a bathroom or laundry.

Choose a simple plastic litter box that the cat will fit in comfortably. Use unscented commercial litter about 4 in (10 cm) deep. If your cat will not use litter, try sand or soil. Clean waste out of the box daily, change the litter at least once a week, and wash out the box with diluted bleach (rinse thoroughly).

Spraying

Spraying is not limited to males. But females rarely spray indoors unless under stress — for example, a medical condition, a change in routine, the addition of a new baby or animal into the household, the appearance of a strange cat, moving home or unfamiliar visitors. If possible, solve the problem by eliminating the cause of the stress. Consult your veterinarian for advice.

There are no reliable methods for stopping tom cats spraying, although you can discourage them from using particular places with water spray (if you catch them in the act), or by aversion techniques (such as serving their food near where they spray).

Notes

Scratching

It is normal for your cat to scratch. Scratching removes worn coverings from its claws, it's good exercise and enjoyable. Provide a substitute scratching surface — something that has the right texture. Pet stores sell vertical posts wrapped in coarse rope; alternatively, a bark-covered log or a post will do. It should be high enough to allow the cat to stretch out. Take the cat to the scratching post at the first sign that it is contemplating the furniture.

Notes

Cat flaps

At first take the cat to the hole and leave the flap open. Once it has jumped through several times, wedge the flap open slightly until it is used to pushing it open.

Leash training

Walking your cat on a leash in mild weather is highly recommended. But it is only successful if the training has begun when the kitten is young. Older cats will not tolerate a leash.

A cat routine

Cats like routines. They feel secure if they know when to expect food and bedtimes, and like to feel they will be played with and groomed regularly.

Feeding time — Provide nourishing meals at regular times for your cat.

Playtime — Play should be encouraged. Spend at least 10 to 15 minutes every day playing with your cat.

Toilet time — If your cat uses a toilet area outside, always let it out when it wakes, after meals and before bedtime.

Bedtime — Cats sleep for up to 16 hours a day and need a quiet spot for their bed.

Year 1

As your kitten grows into a mature cat, and as its body shape changes, so does its behaviour. Keep a year-by-year log of its cat language, its adventures and its funny habits, alongside its weight, measurements and regular worming treatments and a detailed health record of vaccinations, illnesses and special treatments filled in by your veterinarian.

Health record

Vaccinations

Due date	Date given	Vaccine type	Batch no.	Veterinarian signature

Treatment

Date	Treatment

Vital statistics

Date	Weight	Height	Body length

Health notes

Year 2

Health record

Vaccinations

Due date	Date given	Vaccine type	Batch no.	Veterinarian signature

Treatment

Date	Treatment		

Vital statistics

Date	Weight	Height	Body length

Health notes

Year 3

Health record

Vaccinations

Due date	Date given	Vaccine type	Batch no.	Veterinarian signature

Treatment

Date	Treatment

Vital statistics

Date	Weight	Height	Body length

Health notes

Year 4

Health Record

Vaccinations

Due date	Date given	Vaccine type	Batch no.	Veterinarian signature

Treatment

Date	Treatment

Vital statistics

Date	Weight	Height	Body length

Health notes

Year 5

Health record

Vaccinations

Due date	Date given	Vaccine type	Batch no.	Veterinarian signature

Treatment

Date	Treatment

Vital statistics

Date	Weight	Height	Body length

Health notes

Year 6

Health record

Vaccinations

Due date	Date given	Vaccine type	Batch no.	Veterinarian signature

Treatment

Date	Treatment

Vital statistics

Date	Weight	Height	Body length

Health notes

Year 7

Health record

Vaccinations

Due date	Date given	Vaccine type	Batch no.	Veterinarian signature

Treatment

Date	Treatment

Vital statistics

Date	Weight	Height	Body length

Health notes

Year 8

Health Record

Vaccinations

Due date	Date given	Vaccine type	Batch no.	Veterinarian signature

Treatment

Date	Treatment

Vital statistics

Date	Weight	Height	Body length

Health notes

Year 9

Health record

Vaccinations

Due date	Date given	Vaccine type	Batch no.	Veterinarian signature

Treatment

Date	Treatment

Vital statistics

Date	Weight	Height	Body length

Health notes

Year 10

Health record

Vaccinations

Due date	Date given	Vaccine type	Batch no.	Veterinarian signature

Treatment

Date	Treatment

Vital statistics

Date	Weight	Height	Body length

Health notes

Year 11

Health record

Vaccinations

Due date	Date given	Vaccine type	Batch no.	Veterinarian signature

Treatment

Date	Treatment

Vital statistics

Date	Weight	Height	Body length

Health notes

Year 12

Health Record

Vaccinations

Due date	Date given	Vaccine type	Batch no.	Veterinarian signature

Treatment

Date	Treatment

Vital statistics

Date	Weight	Height	Body length

Health notes

Year 13

Health record

Vaccinations

Due date	Date given	Vaccine type	Batch no.	Veterinarian signature

Treatment

Date	Treatment

Vital statistics

Date	Weight	Height	Body length

Health notes

Year 14

Health record

Vaccinations

Due date	Date given	Vaccine type	Batch no.	Veterinarian signature

Treatment

Date	Treatment

Vital statistics

Date	Weight	Height	Body length

Health notes

Year 15

Health record

Vaccinations

Due date	Date given	Vaccine type	Batch no.	Veterinarian signature

Treatment

Date	Treatment

Vital statistics

Date	Weight	Height	Body length

Health notes

Year 16

Health Record

Vaccinations

Due date	Date given	Vaccine type	Batch no.	Veterinarian signature

Treatment

Date	Treatment

Vital statistics

Date	Weight	Height	Body length

Health notes

Year 17

Health record

Vaccinations

Due date	Date given	Vaccine type	Batch no.	Veterinarian signature

Treatment

Date	Treatment

Vital statistics

Date	Weight	Height	Body length

Health notes

Year 18

Health record

Vaccinations

Due date	Date given	Vaccine type	Batch no.	Veterinarian signature

Treatment

Date	Treatment

Vital statistics

Date	Weight	Height	Body length

Health notes

Year 19

Health record

Vaccinations

Due date	Date given	Vaccine type	Batch no.	Veterinarian signature

Treatment

Date	Treatment

Vital statistics

Date	Weight	Height	Body length

Health notes

Year 20

Health Record

Vaccinations

Due date	Date given	Vaccine type	Batch no.	Veterinarian signature

Treatment

Date	Treatment

Vital statistics

Date	Weight	Height	Body length

Health notes

Parts of a cat

Along with humans, cats are mammals. Our basic body structures are similar, with common features such as tissues, organs, hair and mammary glands. However, the cat is a quadruped (four-legged mammal) and a carnivorous (meat-eating) predator.

The tail

The tail, which is part of the spine, is used for balance and serves an important role in communication.

The spine

The spine is held together by muscles (rather than ligaments) and it has up to 26 more vertebrae than humans, giving the back great flexibility. The cat has no collarbone, and it has a shoulder-joint that allows its front legs to turn in almost any direction.

The brain

The areas of the brain associated with the senses are highly developed. The 'intelligence' parts in the frontal lobes are much simpler than those of humans.

The eyes

Cats possess binocular vision — they see the same image in both eyes at the same time. The retina contains a large number of rods (light sensors), allowing them to see in the dark (but not in total darkness). They have less cones (colour sensors) than humans, so do not distinguish colours as well. A layer of cells beneath the retina acts as a mirror and reflects light back on to the retina — this is why cats' eyes 'glow' in the dark. A third eyelid, a membrane, rests at the inner corner of the eye; if the eye needs protection (during a cat fight, for instance), it will unfold over the surface.

The ears

A cat's hearing is much more sensitive than that of a human's. The cone-shaped flap on the ear (a *pinna*) channels sound waves to the inner ear. The *pinna* contains muscles that allow the cat to rotate its ears in a wide arc, picking up sounds.

The nose

Its well-developed sense of smell signals danger, meal times, prey, other cats' territories, and information about the opposite sex.

The whiskers

Whiskers are sensors, sending messages to the brain. Besides the upper whiskers on the cheeks and above the eyes, there are four rows on the upper lip — they help guide a cat in total darkness. Whiskers on the forelegs sense movement of prey held under the front paws.

The mouth

The 30 permanent teeth — 16 in the upper jaw and 14 in the lower — come through when the cat is between three and six months. Canine teeth are for biting, and blade-like molar teeth for shearing flesh. The cat has short, sturdy jaws with powerful muscles. The tongue is covered with tiny backward-facing barbs.

Temperature — between 101.5 and 102.5°F (38.6 and 39.2°C). When stressed, a cat's temperature may rise.

Heart beat — averages from 120 to 240 beats per minute. The heart-beat rate increases during physical activity and when the cat is stressed, afraid or excited.

Respiratory rate — average about 20 to 30 breaths per minute when resting, about twice the average rate of humans.

Blood — three types: A, B and AB (which is very rare).

Weight — an average adult cat weighs between 9-12 lb (4-5 kg).

Cat moves

Cats are extraordinarily graceful animals. Agile and fast, they have the ability to climb great heights, balance on the narrowest of ledges, sprint like Olympic champions and fall on to their feet.

Balancing

The cat has a wonderful sense of balance. This is related to the speed with which the ultra-sensitive balancing organ in its inner ear sends messages, via the brain, to its muscles. In turn, the cat's muscle reaction is remarkably fast. The cat can alter its muscles and joints far faster than a human can. The tail also aids the cat's balance. It acts as a counter-weight — for instance, when a cat on a narrow fence turns in one direction, its tail moves in the opposite direction, maintaining its centre of gravity. Likewise, when the cat is running at high speed and turns quickly, the tail swings away from the direction of the body, giving it stability. (However, cats with very short tails, such as Manx cats, also have a great sense of balance.)

Jumping

The cat crouches, tipping back its pelvis and bending its hip, knee and ankle joints to achieve maximum lift-off. Then it contracts its muscles and stretches out its body. It lands on its forelegs then draws in its back legs. In familiar territory, a running or walking cat may go straight into a jump without missing a step. The average cat can jump about five times its own height — and some can land on the narrowest of spaces.

Running

A great sprinter, the cat is fast over short distances. Covering about three times its body length in each leap at full speed (about 30 mph, or 50 kph), it has the necessary quickness and agility for hunting, but will fade within a few hundred yards. When it runs, the cat uses its highly flexible spine like a spring, stretching its trunk fully and extending its limbs in the air. Its hunting prowess is enhanced by the ability to jump, twist, and brake dramatically — it can stop and freeze in mid-step. However, it is not good at suddenly changing direction.

Climbing

The cat has powerful back and hind leg muscles, which give it the strength and agility to climb with great ease. Most climbs begin with a jump to gain height. The cat stretches its limbs and extends its hooked claws, which grip like climbers' crampons. The clawed feet power the cat upwards, hold after hold. The cat is less graceful when climbing down — it tends to slide down backwards, then turn to leap to the ground. Although all cats possess climbing ability, some enjoy heights more than others.

Falling

When a cat falls, its eyes and inner ear transmit information to the brain to correctly position its body for landing. It alters its body position to cushion the landing — arching its back and extending its legs. Spongy pads on its paws, which are covered in tough skin, act as shock absorbers when the cat lands. The higher the fall, the more time the cat has to relax its body and correctly position itself for landing — and the less likely it is to get hurt.

Sleeping

Cats are great sleepers. An adult cat, in good physical condition and fully active, will spend between 16 and 18 hours a day asleep. Kittens spend most of their first month in deep sleep, and older cats may sleep for up to 80 percent of the time. The cat's sleeping pattern is different from that of humans. It takes a series of 'cat-naps', sleeping for short stretches. Like humans, the cat has a number of levels of sleep — from drowsiness to deep sleep. During light sleep, the cat's muscles are not completely relaxed and it awakens quickly at the slightest sound. You can pick up a cat without disturbing it when it is in the deep-sleep stage — its body is so relaxed. And, according to researchers, during periods of deep sleep the cat's brain activity is similar to that of dreaming humans.

Cat language

What exactly is going on in that cat mind? Your cat gives you a few very clear signals about its moods — eyes, ears, tail and whiskers are all powerful signs of pleasure, anger, fear, unhappiness, and so on.

Eyes
: Open wide — polite interest of a relaxed, but alert, cat.
Open very wide — startled.
Open, 'hard' and intensely focused — in stalking mode.
Eyes narrow and pupils focused — ready to lash out.
Unblinking stare — alert and curious.
Pupils narrowed to vertical slits — reacting to bright sunlight.
Pupils widened to large black pools — reacting to darkness.

Nose
: Twitching — curiosity, on the scent of prey.
Nostrils wide — on the alert.

Ears
: Up and slightly forward — relaxed and moderately alert.
Upright — on full alert.
Straight forward — in stalking mode, listening intensely for hidden prey.
Slightly downwards and to the side — irritation, fright or possibly submission.
Flattened — sign of aggression, about to lash out.
Twitching — anxiety.

Tail
: Held high with the tail bent slightly forward — happy and confident, used in greeting.
Flicking from side to side — in a state of tension.
Held horizontal — relaxed.
Held low — uncertain.
Tucked under — very tense.
Lashing from side to side — agitated.

Whiskers & fur
: Whiskers forward and fanned out — alert, curious or angry.
Whiskers sideways and closer together — relaxed.
Whiskers back and tight together — frightened.
Fur standing on end — scared or angry.

Cat stances

Happy — erect tail, alert expression with ears pricked forward.

Anxious — body tense and crouched low, pupils dilated.

Aggressive — arched back, stiff tail upright, fur fluffed up, ears forward and flat against the head.

Defensive stance no. 1 — crouching in a ball, hair flattened, whiskers back, ears downwards and to the side, eyes very wide.

Defensive stance no. 2 — rolling on back, showing teeth, claws out ready to defend.

Cat lexicon

Voice

Cats use their voices along with body language and territorial marking (see page 69) to communicate with humans and with other cats. A cat's vocabulary is quite extensive. It can be divided into three main groups:

- Low-intensity sounds, such as soft contented murmurs (purrs) made in peaceful situations with the mouth closed.
- Vowel pattern sounds (various meows), which are clear sounds made with the mouth opening and closing rapidly; the cat uses different vowels for different situations.
- High-intensity sounds (demands and cries), full growls, snarls, hisses and various loud cries.

Vocabulary

Purring — a low-frequency sound produced somewhere deep in the chest (not by the vocal chords); usually a sign of pleasure or contentment, but may indicate nervousness or pain.

Chirping — a soft, bird-like greeting.

Acknowledgement — a short murmur, a response to hearing its name or antici-pating something positive (such as getting fed).

Meowing — expresses a variety of moods, but most often the cat is offering an invitation to feed or cuddle it.

Strange and 'purrfect' behaviour

Freezing in mid-step — locating prey or identifying danger.

Rolling on the ground — playing, or in a defensive position.

Arching the back — having a stretch; also responding to a threat.

Hunching on ground, body tense, hind soles flat, front paws drawn back below shoulders, tail tip twitching slightly, head forward — about to spring on prey or another cat.

Rubbing against something or somebody — being affectionate; also marking out territory with the secretions of glands around the face.

Rapid chattering — excitement, usually generated by an out-of-reach bird, or for a tom the sight of a potential mate.

Calling — females use it to signal readiness to mate and males to coax females; also used by toms announcing readiness to fight.

Mating calls — the female uses a two-syllable call; the male answers with a 'mowl'-like sound.

Snarling — short, intense aggressive sound usually made during fighting.

Hissing and/or spitting — aggression, often accompanied by a menacing quick slap on the ground with a paw.

Demanding — a high-intensity, persistent sound.

Complaining — well-tuned and high-pitched.

Bewilderment — a loud cry of confusion.

Growling — steady, low-pitched sound, frightened or angry.

Caterwauling — fight about to commence.

Screaming — intense pain.

Territory

Territory is a big issue for your cat. Every cat has its own special area and some cats have up to three. Two of these will be private areas, and one a communal ground, like a village green, where cats come and go regularly and meet their friends and acquaintances.

The first, or principal, territory is the cat's private den or lair. This is where the cat sleeps, and it takes any challenges to this area very seriously — it will fight hard to defend this space against any intruders. The second space is for living in, a territory that will be shared with other animals in its household. Intrusions by visiting cats and dogs will be resented and possibly repelled. The third — communal — territory is claimed by cats with a liking for exploring their neighbourhoods and ones that love to roam around at night. This is not a place for confrontations. Rather, it is for hunting and meeting. Observe your cat closely - you should be able to identfy the boundaries of these areas, and even track favoured routes.

Defence of the territory

A neutered tom will be content with a much smaller private lair than an unneutered male or a mother with kittens. Although the living area is for social interaction, and is not defended as strongly, two or more cats are likely to engage in power struggles within the territory. And for good reason — cats who dominate others not only have more space but also feed first.

Night life

Domestic cats who are not kept indoors at night congregate together, usually on a piece of neutral ground or sometimes a rooftop. Observers have recorded similar activity among tigers. The cats seem to come together to engage in social activity. They converse, groom each other and play. The gathering breaks up sometime before dawn when they all return home for a cat nap.

Friends not enemies

Not all cat relationships are about power. Cats develop social preferences: they have playmates, grooming companions, and 'friends' they like to sleep near.

Marking territory

Cats possess scent glands on the forehead, around the mouth, the paw pads and anus. These glands produce chemicals called pheromones. Cats use scent to mark territory, and as a way of recognizing and communicating with each other. The smell provides other cats with information on the sex of the cat that left the marking, on whether or not it was neutered, and even on its state of health and temper.

Rubbing The pheromones produced during facial rubbing have a calming effect and are usually reserved for marking in, or close to, the cat's lair. Rubbing is friendly, social behaviour, and many cats who live together will often rub each other in passing. When your cat rubs, or 'bunts', its head against your face, it is showing you love and affection.

Spraying The most obvious (and, to you, the most irritating) way a cat marks its territory. The cat sprays the urine at nose-level, making it convenient for another cat to pick up the scent. Spraying also allows the cat to cover a wide area.

Scratching Cats also use their claws to mark their territories and places within them, such as furniture and trees. Whenever the cat scratches on such objects, glands between its toes secrete a scent, leaving olfactory marks as well as visual ones.

Hunting

By nature, your cat is a predator, and if it were living in the wild it would live off prey it had hunted down and killed. You can observe hunting behaviour in kittens. They learn to lie in wait, pounce suddenly, use their paws to toy with mouse-sized objects and practise the bite to the neck that immobilizes prey. Although your well-fed cat does not need to hunt, the instinct is still very strong. Hunting is done for pleasure and the endearing habit of bringing you their kills is the feline version of gift-giving, of saying they love you.

Cat care

A few vital things — establishing a regular grooming and worming routine, finding a good veterinarian, getting annual health checks and keeping vaccinations up to date, and deciding whether and when to neuter — can make all the difference to your cat's long-term health and happiness.

Grooming

Cats spend hours licking their fur, using their tongue with its rows of backward-pointing hooks (*papillae*) as a comb for raking the skin and fur. Nevertheless, all cats, especially longhairs, need extra grooming.

Use a soft bristle brush and a wide-toothed metal comb. Be systematic and gentle, and groom all parts of the body, including the belly and under the paws and tail. Grooming helps to prevent hairballs by removing dead hair. This is particularly important for longhairs. In grooming itself the cat will ingest hair, which will gradually accumulate into a hairball and may cause an obstruction.

If you find knots and matted areas, brush or comb them gently, making sure you are not hurting the cat. If the fur is badly matted, you may need to take the cat to a vet.

Use a fine-toothed comb to go over the coat for fleas. Treat fleas with a commercial flea powder or spray — make sure that any preparation you use is suitable for cats.

Remove stains or grease with a piece of cotton dampened in alcohol (take care to avoid the eyes). Bathe the cat only if it is very dirty — and do it in a warm room.

Check for signs of dirt or discharge in the ears or inner corners of the eyes. If necessary, clean the ears with cotton wool moistened with almond or olive oil (never insert cotton buds in the ears), and wash the eyes with a warm, weak solution of salt and water.

Check the teeth for a build-up of tartar (once formed, it will need to be removed by a veterinarian), and the claws (which may need to be clipped — consult your vet).

Once grooming has been completed, rub bay rum conditioner into the fur — it will bring up the gloss and highlight the colour of the cat's coat.

Choosing a veterinarian

Find a veterinarian in your locality before you have an emergency. Ask cat-owning friends, breeders, cat fancy association, or local humane society for recommendations. Choose a vet with an after-hours service that can deal with emergencies. You need to feel that the vet is comfortable handling your animal. Remember regular check-ups, vaccinations and prompt attention when your cat gets sick or injured can save a great deal of heartache.

Vaccinations

Vaccination is a preventative measure against serious infections. Your vet will recommend the most suitable for your cat. Kittens are not protected by the vaccine until about 10 days after the first vaccination. Keep them indoors during this period. If you are not sure a new kitten has been vaccinated, have it re-vaccinated. An extra vaccination will not be harmful.

Make sure your veterinarian records — and signs — all vaccination details in this book. Take *Cat-a-Log* with you for endorsing when you go for annual boosters and also when you take your cat to a breeder or cat hotel.

Worming

Worm your cat when you get it, then at regular intervals after that. Young cats should be treated every two weeks to age five months, then every six to eight weeks until they are one year old, then six-monthly. Consult your vet for advice.

Neutering

If you are not planning to breed from a female, consult your vet about having it spayed. This is usually done between three and four months. Spaying, a very safe operation performed under general anaesthetic, involves the removal of both ovaries and much of the uterus.

It is generally recommended that a male cat should be neutered when it is fully mature at around eight months old, before it begins spraying. The testicles are removed under general anaesthetic. Recovery should be fast.

A healthy diet

A cat can be very demanding to feed. A kitten requires four or five small meals a day, and a mature cat two or three small meals, rather than a single big breakfast or dinner. The diet must be balanced, and contain protein, fats and carbohydrates.

The cat is also a very fussy eater. Its highly developed senses of smell and taste allow it to detect food that is less than fresh, and it will reject food if it does not smell right or is served at the wrong temperature. Being a creature of habit, the cat likes to be fed at the same time each day, and in the same place.

Basic rules

- Do not feed a cat raw fish or raw pork.
- Feed raw meat (excluding pork) if your cat likes it.
- Avoid bones except large knuckle bones — always remove any small bones from fish and chicken.
- Egg yolks may be served raw or cooked, but cook egg whites.
- Only serve pasta, potatoes and rice if they are cooked.
- Feed commercial cat food from reputable manufacturers only.
- Serve food at room temperature.
- Do not give a cat food that is intended for a dog or other animals.
- Do not give a cat any food that is even slightly spoiled.
- Dispose of uneaten food at the end of each meal.
- Keep feeding bowls and utensils clean.
- Do not let your cat overeat.

Nutritional foods

Cats are carnivores, not vegetarians. They can digest some vegetable matter (preferably cooked) but are unable to live long on a meat-free diet. Commercial cat foods are available in three main forms: canned meat, semi-moist pellets in foil bags and dried pellets. Choose food from reputable producers, which are carefully balanced to meet cats' special dietary needs at various stages of life, and include essential minerals and vitamins. Special formulae with different proportions of protein are available for kittens, adult cats and 'senior' cats (aged seven years and over). It is much more difficult to feed your cat a balanced diet that consists mainly of fresh foods. Hit-or-miss table scraps are usually insufficient; equally, an all-protein diet is unhealthy for a cat at any age. Supplement fresh foods with vitamins and minerals.

Most cats enjoy chewing on grass, so make sure any chemicals or fertilizer used on your lawn are non-toxic. Whatever types of food you choose, it is always best to vary the diet. And be ready to adjust the diet to satisfy the cat's eating habits — it will let you know if it doesn't like the food you are providing. Consult a vet if your cat has refused food for 48 hours — don't worry too much if the cat has the occasional fasting day.

Likes

Dislikes

Weight

An average adult cat should weigh about 9-12 lb (4-5 kg). An overweight cat will have a large abdomen that hangs down, and its breathing will be laboured. Obesity is usually due to overfeeding and/or lack of exercise. If your cat is overweight, consult a vet to make sure the excess weight is not caused by a medical problem.

Liquids

Although a cat gets much of the moisture it requires from its food, it is important that fresh water is always available. Despite the mythology, many cats do not drink milk or cream.

Health care

You will usually be the first to detect anything wrong with your cat. Contact the vet at the first signs of sickness - most would prefer to answer a false alarm than be called in too late. It is better to seek advice early rather than late. If diagnosed early enough, most diseases can be treated. If you are worried or unsure what to do, call up the vet and discuss your worries.

Emergencies

Call the veterinarian immediately if a cat:
- is in a state of shock, or hemorrhaging
- is partly or completely unconscious
- is obviously injured
- has been bitten by a snake or spider
- is falling over, uncoordinated or partly or completely paralysed
- is vomiting frequently or has had severe diarrhoea for several hours
- has had contact with a poison (if possible, take the poison with you so the vet can administer the correct treatment immediately).

Signs of ill health

- Behavioural changes — depression; irritability; trembling; breaking routines; excessive sleeping; becoming more active; excessive grooming, licking, biting or scratching.

- Temperature — if the cat's temperature is below 100.5°F (38°C) or above 104.5°F (40°C), consult a veterinarian immediately (normal temperature is between 101.5 and 102.5°F/38.6 and 39.2°C).

- Pain — any obvious signs, including restlessness, crying, stillness, changes in physical activity.
- Swelling.
- Eyes — redness or gummy; changes in pupil size; discoloration; abnormal movements, lack of response to visual stimuli.
- Ears — dirty and/or presence of discharge; unpleasant smell; lack of response to sounds.
- Nose — dry, dull and warm; cracked.
- Breathing — laboured; coughing; sneezing or wheezing; heavy breathing when resting accompanied by nostrils dilating at every breath; change in voice.
- Mouth and gums — dribbling; inflammation of mouth or gums; breath smelling like urine.

- Eating and drinking — loss or increase in appetite; excessive drinking; difficulty in chewing or swallowing; regurgitating or vomiting food.
- Abrupt weight change — gain or loss.
- Vomiting — frequent vomiting should be investigated.
- Fur and skin — matted, greasy, thinning and hair loss; dandruff, scabs or inflamed areas.
- Abdomen — enlarged.
- Limbs — obvious pain; lameness; limb being carried or dragged; changes in habits relating to movement; loss of balance.
- Defecation and urination — changes in the consistency of faeces, such as diarrhoea or constipation; straining; increased frequency; presence of blood.

Picking up a sick cat

The sick cat is often difficult to handle — it resists efforts to pick it up in order to avoid pain or discomfort. Approach it slowly and calmly. Pick it up by the scruff of the neck, and support its body weight with your arm under its hind legs. To avoid being scratched by its front claws, carry it at arm's length.

Nursing a sick cat

It is difficult to nurse a cat, who cannot tell you how it is feeling. The cat's behaviour will be different from normal — it may be passive and exhibit no reactions, or it may strike out with its claws and/or teeth. You will need to be patient and gentle. Most cats respond to love and affection, although don't overwhelm it with attention. Care for the cat in a quiet, peaceful environment. Be careful that children do not stress it.

Keep it clean, warm and comfortable. Maintain adequate food and drink supplies and, if necessary, help it to eat and drink. Make sure its feeding and water bowls are clean and keep them away from other household equipment. Help it with grooming and cleaning where necessary.

Always wash your hands both before and after handling a sick cat so that you don't transmit any disease or infection to or from the cat. If necessary, isolate the sick cat from other animals.

Administering pills

Cats don't like taking pills. If you find that your cat resists your attempts, there are several strategies you can try. One is to crush up the tablet and hide it in normal food. Or if your cat likes cheese, you can disguise the crushed pill in a little ball of cream cheese, which is sticky and once touched must be licked up.

Games cats play

Learning to play teaches kittens essential skills they need to survive — jumping, ambushing, biting, catching imaginary prey, chasing, controlling objects held in its paws, play-fighting. At around six months old, it leaves kitten games behind and becomes a little more serious.

Even so, most cats can be encouraged to play, especially if there are cat companions in the same household. Provide some cat toys, such as catnip mice, bouncy balls, ping-pong balls, feathers, rubber mice and bones, and balls of wool (but always supervise a cat playing with wool).

Keep a record of your cat's favourite games and pastimes.

Favourite kitten games

Favourite cat games
(from age of six months)

Travel

Cats don't like travelling very much. You really can't blame them. They are confined in a 'cat carrier', denied the right to hunt or stretch very far and don't get to cuddle up to someone warm. So indulge your travelling cat, fuss over it and make sure you treat it right.

Cat carriers

Cats need to travel in carriers — even on short trips in cars. Choose a carrier that will be safe and will protect the cat during the journey. Make it comfortable and familiar — add your cat's favourite toys and a blanket if the weather's cold; in hot weather the carrier should be covered with a damp cloth. When putting the cat into its carrier, pick it up with your arms around its hind legs, and keep your grip on the cat until just before you secure the door.

Moving home

Keep the cat in a quiet room while everything is being moved out to prevent it from becoming scared and running off. On arrival at your new home, let the cat get used to its surroundings but keep it confined to the house for at least five days.

Car sense

- Don't let a cat travel loose in a car — it may become upset or get in the driver's way and cause an accident.
- Never leave a cat unattended in a car on a hot day — it may get overheated.
- Don't feed the cat just before the journey, particularly if it's a bad traveller.

Special travel arrangements

Contact the airline, bus, railroad or shipping line well in advance of travel as it may have special regulations. Find out when and where you must check in your cat and what papers — health certificates and so on — you need to bring.

Check with your veterinarian that your cat is in good health suitable for travel. (A pregnant or nursing queen and young kittens should not be taken on long journeys.) Although it is not advisable to sedate a cat for travelling, a veterinarian can prescribe a tranquilizer if the cat is nervous.

Some airlines allow cats in the passenger cabin as long as its carrier fits in the space beneath the seat (there may be a limit on the number of animals in the cabin, so make travel arrangements well in advance). If your cat is not allowed in the cabin, it flies in a pressurized cargo hold.

The cat must be transported in a carrier approved by the airline. The carrier should be sturdy and light with plenty of ventilation, and just large enough for the cat to stand up and turn around in. It must have a lockable door — make sure it's secured firmly before checking the cat in.

The cat will need food, water and access to a litter tray. Instructions for feeding and watering and name and contact phone numbers (at both ends of the journey) should be clearly marked on the carrier.

Travelling between countries

In order to prevent the spread of rabies, strict regulations apply to transporting cats between various countries of the world — check regulations carefully before you decide on your cat's travel schedule. (Airlines can give you details of regulations and requirements.)

The cat may need to have specific injections and certificates for entry into some countries.

A cat taken overseas may have to spend time in quarantine on entry into some countries or on return to its home country.

Travel log

Date	Destination	Mode of travel	Comments

Travel log

Date	Destination	Mode of travel	Comments

Travel log

Date	Destination	Mode of travel	Comments

Cat hotels

Sometimes, when you go away for vacation or work, you have to leave your cat behind. Then, you'll have to send it to a cattery — in other words, a cat hotel. Finding the right one is a case of detective work: ask your friends for recommendations.

Visit the cattery in advance to make sure it has sympathetic, knowledgeable staff, is clean, has adequate space, and will cater for any special requirements (for example, diet or medication). Find out about its provisions for on-call veterinary services.

Any reputable cat hotel will not take cats who have not been immunized — you will have to show up-to-date vaccination records. You may need to make reservations well in advance, especially in holiday seasons.

Date	Name of cattery	Comments

Date	Name of cattery	Comments

Cat shows and organizations

Yours is the most beautiful, intelligent, funny cat in the world. No wonder you want to display it to the universe. You may want to enter your cat in cat shows — the beauty contests of the feline world — and/or join the appropriate cat fancy association for your cat.

Cat fancy associations

These are the organizations that draw up the rules and regulations for the various breeds of cats, and provide registration for, and information about, pedigree and other cats. Many of these associations also sponsor cat shows. To obtain details of a local cat fancy association, contact your veterinarian or local pet store.

Cat shows

Entering your cat in a show involves a great deal of time and effort. A show may be for pedigreed cats only, or particular breeds, or it may be open to all kinds of cats. If you are interested in showing your cat, contact the local cat fancy association to find out how to enter, and the competition conditions. Many cat fancy associations will be able to help the beginner with advice on what will be expected at the show and how to prepare your cat for it.

Results

Date	Name of Show	Comments

Results

Date	Name of Show	Comments

The pregnant cat

Besides being an exciting event, when your cat becomes pregnant and has kittens it is a time of responsibility. You must give her a healthy diet, pamper her and help prepare for the birth.

Breeding

If your cat is a particular breed and you are interested in breeding, then contact the cat fancy association for that specific breed. It will be able to provide you with up-to-date, relevant information. If you don't know the address of the association, ask your vet or local pet store.

Stages of pregnancy

- The cat's appetite increases.
- At about 21 days after mating the nipples are slightly enlarged and bright pink.
- Between 36 and 45 days, the cat begins to get larger around the middle, and the kittens' skeletons will be visible on an X-ray.
- After about nine weeks, or between 63 and 65 days, the cat will be ready to give birth.

Looking after a pregnant cat

Feed her a well-balanced diet rich in calcium.

You may find a good place for a nest, where the kittens will be born and spend their first few weeks of life. Or your cat may prefer to choose a place a week or so before the kittens are born. Make sure it is clean.

As she gets closer to giving birth, the cat's behaviour may change — which may range from high spirits to extreme quiet. Unless she is hyper-active (in which case, consult a vet), the best thing is to let her be.

The birth

In the hours before birth, the mother may display nervous behaviour — for instance, she may be anxious, restless, wash herself continuously, scratch or pace.

The most reliable indicator of the onset of labour is the movement of her sides, due to contractions of the uterus. When this happens, don't let her outside. She will lie down and begin to pant when the contractions become more violent. It is generally 30 to 60 minutes from the onset of labour until the first kitten is born.

You can expect three to five kittens. The kittens are usually born at intervals of five to 90 minutes. As each kitten is born, the mother breaks the birth sac surrounding it, clears away the passages around the kitten's nose and mouth, breaks the umbilical cord connecting her to the kitten and licks the newborn. The afterbirth, which is expelled five to 15 minutes after the birth, is usually eaten by the mother — it provides her with nourishment.

Assisting the birth

Provide the cat with a bowl of water — giving birth is thirsty work. Leave her alone as long as she seems to be handling the birth well. If she fails to break the birth sac, you must do it (otherwise the kitten will not be able to breathe), and then clean the kitten's mouth and nose with a clean cloth. Make sure that for each kitten there is an afterbirth — it may cause infection if it is not expelled.

If the cat is straining hour after hour without giving birth, or if a kitten gets stuck and/or is head first, consult a vet immediately. Try to calm the mother, who may get frantic.

If a kitten is not breathing, wrap it in a clean cloth (it will be slippery). Holding it firmly with its head down, swing it gently in an arc then stop suddenly — any mucus blocking the air passages should be pushed out. If that is unsuccessful, rub its ribs vigorously (but do not push) to stimulate breathing. Failing that, try artificial respiration.

After the birth

The mother begins nursing soon after the kittens are born. Never remove her kittens, unless she is ignoring them. Give the cat family peace and quiet, and do not allow many visitors. Let small children look but not touch.

The feeding mother's diet should be rich in calcium (preferably via cow's or goat's milk), proteins and fats. Allow her as much food as she wants. If the mother stops eating 24 hours after giving birth, if she has a temperature above 103°F (39.4°C), or if she will neither groom nor nurse her kittens, call your veterinarian immediately.

It is possible for a nursing cat to be in heat, sometimes as early as one week after giving birth.

Newborn kittens

The newborn kitten is extremely fragile. It weighs only about 4 oz (100 g) and its bones and motor skills have not been developed. For the first 10 days, it can barely stand. It cannot see or hear until it is three or four weeks old. The kitten needs time to get used to the world, and to learn how to live in it with human beings. Unless the mother is unable to care for her kittens, or has rejected one or more of them, there is little for you to do after birth except to help with weaning and providing a clean, safe environment.

Dangers

Kittens are susceptible to chills and respiratory infections, so you must make sure that their environment is free of draughts. Their nest should be kept warm — at around 75-80°F (24-27°C).

Make sure that the kittens are not in danger of being trampled underfoot once they can crawl or walk.

A young kitten is small and extremely fragile and should be handled as little as possible. If you do pick up a kitten, do it securely, supporting the full body with one hand under its chest and the other under its back legs. Never pick up a kitten by the scruff of its neck; it is precarious and slippery and it may cause pain. Do not allow children near the kittens without supervision.

Do not take a kitten out in cold weather. And do not bathe it until it is at least six months old, preferably a year — if at all.

Feeding

A newborn kitten gets a substance called colostrum from its mother's nipples. This protects it against infection until it builds up its own resistance; without it, the kitten is susceptible to feline enteritis.

Watch the kittens suckling — it is important that all the kittens, and especially those born small, are getting enough to eat. For those kittens who are missing out or are orphaned, bottle-feed with milk formulas specially for young kittens — serve it slowly, at room temperature — and give them a suitable vitamin-mineral supplement (following directions on label). If you are unsure, you can consult your vet on the kitten's nutritional needs. Never feed bones to the young kitten (or to a mature cat).

If all goes well, there will be nothing for you to do. The mother will feed the kittens until weaning begins. Start to wean the kitten, very gradually, from the third week. Provide water for the weaning kitten after each meal.

House-training

Apart from providing a good-sized litter box and keeping it clean, leave this to the mother. Once trained, most kittens keep themselves meticulously clean.

Sexing the kittens

The female kitten's anus and vulva are very close together. In a male, the anus and penis are further apart.

Finding suitable homes

Inevitably, you will have to find suitable homes for some, if not all, of the kittens. It is your responsibility to do everything you can to make sure that the kittens will be well looked after and loved. You may find good homes through:

- Friends and acquaintances — probably the best source. You will know the household, and may be able to check on the kittens' progress from time to time.
- Your veterinarian — your vet may have clients offering good homes to kittens.
- Cat fanciers' organizations — if your kitten is pedigreed, notify the secretary of the appropriate breed society that you have kittens for sale.
- Pet stores — only choose a pet store that keeps kittens in clean, hygienic conditions, and shows genuine interest.
- Humane or cat welfare organizations — these are usually staffed by genuinely concerned cat lovers. But remember that if no-one offers the kitten a new home, it may have to be put down.

Record of litters

Record the details of your cat's litters here, and keep notes about her condition and those of the kittens. You can also keep a record of the kittens' new homes. Use any unfilled pages for your favourite cat photographs.

Date of birth

Sire/s (if known)

Number of kittens   female   male

Notes (record the sex, colouring, condition, development and new home of each kitten)

Date of birth

Sire/s (if known)

Number of kittens   female   male

Notes (record the sex, colouring, condition, development and new home of each kitten)

Date of birth

Sire/s (if known)

Number of kittens   female   male

Notes (record the sex, colouring, condition, development and new home of each kitten)

Date of birth

Sire/s (if known)

Number of kittens   female   male

Notes (record the sex, colouring, condition, development and new home of each kitten)

Date of birth

Sire/s (if known)

Number of kittens   female   male

Notes (record the sex, colouring, condition, development and new home of each kitten)

Date of birth

Sire/s (if known)

Number of kittens   female   male

Notes (record the sex, colouring, condition, development and new home of each kitten)

Date of birth

Sire/s (if known)

Number of kittens   female   male

Notes (record the sex, colouring, condition, development and new home of each kitten)

Date of birth

Sire/s (if known)

Number of kittens   female   male

Notes (record the sex, colouring, condition, development and new home of each kitten)

The aging cat

Your cat deserves to enjoy a long life and spend its old age in comfort and serenity. It's not unusual for a cat to live for 15 to 20 years, and there are many ways you can keep it healthy and happy.

When is a cat old?

Like people, you should not treat your cat as old until it indicates — through behaviour or illness — that it is slowing down. Some cats are still as lively and active at 12 or 13 as they were when young. Others seem to 'act old' and begin to lose their vitality when they are only seven or eight. There seems no difference in length of life between male and female, nor between a cat that has been neutered and one that has not.

The aging process

The aging process occurs gradually, over a period of several years. It is likely you won't even notice it happening, unless your cat has a severe illness or accident. As your cat becomes older, it will sleep more, will be less physically active than previously, and will be more prone to respiratory infections such as cat flu.

The cat may begin to behave differently, becoming irritable and less adaptable to change, or it may withdraw altogether. When you see this happening, treat the cat with patience and give it plenty of assurance — it may be suffering from aches and pains, or finding it hard to deal with its inability to perform physical activities that were once second nature. If you cannot identify a particular physical reason for such behavioural changes, consult your vet.

Signs of aging

Some older cats get heavier as their metabolism slows, and they exercise less. Others may suffer from digestive upsets — vomiting, diarrhoea, constipation — that result in weight loss. The gloss and smoothness of the fur begins to disappear, and there is usually a little greying around the nose. The skin and hair becomes drier, and the hair thinner, even bald, in places.

Constipation and digestive upsets may be problems, possibly related to chronic kidney disease (which is common) or heart disease. Other signs include shortness of breath after exertion, lower resistance to disease, loss of muscle tone, and slowness of recovery after illness. Tumours are relatively common; any growth or lump should be investigated.

It is usual to expect a general deterioration of hearing and sight, including problems such as cataracts. Teeth are affected by tartar, general erosion, a loss of enamel, gum infections and teeth loss.

Looking after Your cat for a long life

Your cat has more chance to live a long life if you look after it well from its earliest days as a kitten. Vaccinations and boosters, annual check-ups, and early treatment of illness or injury will prolong your cat's healthy life.

A cat that has enjoyed a good balanced diet all its life will have sound bones, good teeth and excellent muscle tone. As it gets older, alter its diet, serving smaller meals more often, and cutting down on fats and rich red meats: if you serve your cat commercially prepared foods, choose the special 'seniors' food and consult your vet about giving it vitamin-mineral supplements. And make sure that the cat is sleeping in a warm, draught-free place, which will lessen its likelihood of suffering from arthritis and rheumatism.

Groom the cat daily to remove dead hair that could cause skin irritations, keep the eyes and ears free of discharge, make sure the anus area is clean and worm the cat regularly.

Take your cat for six-monthly check-ups once it has reached the age of 10 or 12, or earlier if it is beginning to show signs of slowing down or any of the symptoms of aging described opposite.
And, most importantly, don't forget to pamper your cat. After all, it has been an important member of your family for years, and now it deserves lots of love and affection.

A new cat: companion or rival?

As your cat gets older, you may consider introducing another cat into the house. If you do so, do it discreetly. Your older cat may resent the newcomer, and if it believes it is being ignored in favour of the intruder, its feelings may be hurt. Spend lots of time with it, and give it a great deal of reassurance and affection until it gets used to the new cat. They may even become good friends.

Your cat's final resting place

Inevitably, one day you are going to farewell your dearly loved cat. You may have had time to say a proper goodbye, or your cat may have passed away suddenly. You can only wish that its death was a peaceful one.

Record of your cat's final resting place (if known)

An epitaph (written memorial) for your cat